Sikh GURDWARA

Kanwaljit Kaur Singh

Contents

A & C BLACK • LONDON

A Sikh gurdwara

This book is about a Sikh *gurdwara*, a place where Sikhs meet to worship God. The word *gurdwara* means 'the door of the Guru'. It is the place where the *Guru Granth Sahib*, the holy book of Sikhs is kept.

Sikhism, the religion that Sikhs follow, was started over five hundred years ago by Guru Nanak in India. After Guru Nanak came nine other Gurus. Sikhs believe in the teachings of the Ten Gurus which are written in the *Guru Granth Sahib*.

▲ *Mr Piara Singh and Mr Jagjivan Singh welcomed the children with the Sikh greeting 'Sat Sri Akal', which means 'remember the True and Immortal God'.*

The children in this book visited the Gurdwara Sri Guru Singh Sabha in Hounslow, Middlesex. They wanted to find out more about Sikhism. They were shown round by Mr Piara Singh, the Secretary of the *gurdwara*.

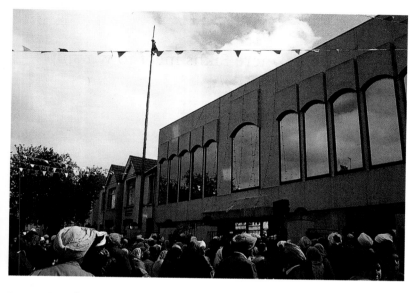

The Nishan Sahib ▼

◄ *The flagpole on the roof of every gurdwara is wrapped in saffron-coloured cloth. The colour saffron symbolises that Sikhs are ready to give up their lives for God.*

Mr Singh pointed out the Sikh flag called the *Nishan Sahib*, flying from the roof of the *gurdwara*. The flag is made of saffron-coloured cloth, with the Sikh *Khanda* symbol in the centre.

The *Khanda* symbol has a sword in the middle, which is sharp on both sides. The sword is a symbol of God's power. The circle is to show that God has no beginning and no end. There are two other swords, which remind Sikhs to serve God by being truthful and by fighting for truth and justice for all.

The children saw that Sikh men wear turbans on their heads. Mr Singh explained that Sikhs who practise their religion do not cut their hair and keep it covered under a turban.

Women keep their un-cut hair tied in a bun at the back of the neck and covered with a long scarf called a *dupatta*.

▲ *Usually, men wear Western clothes and women wear Punjabi clothes to the gurdwara.*

How Sikhism began

Guru Nanak was born in 1469, in Punjab in India. In the Panjabi language the word guru means 'teacher'. Sikhs use the word only for Guru Nanak, his nine successors and the *Guru Granth Sahib*. These are spiritual guides for the Sikhs who teach God's message.

▲ *This map shows the area of India where Sikhism began.*

There are many stories about Guru Nanak's childhood which show that he was not an ordinary child. He was interested in serving people especially those who were poor and needy. At the *gurdwara* the children heard the story of The True Bargain.

Guru Nanak's father, Kalu, gave Nanak 20 rupees and told him to go to the market and buy groceries to sell at a profit in the family shop. 'Make sure you strike a good bargain' he told his son.

On their way to the market, Nanak and his friend Bala saw a group of holy men. Nanak was upset to discover that they had not eaten for days.

On his way back from the market Nanak started giving the food he'd bought to the holy men. Bala tried to stop him, warning Nanak that his father would be very angry. But Nanak paid no heed and the boys returned home empty-handed.

Kalu was furious. 'I told you to spend wisely, to make a good bargain' he shouted. 'I did', replied Nanak. 'Surely, there's no better bargain than feeding the poor'.

During Guru Nanak's time, Indian society was divided between Hindus and Muslims who had very different beliefs from each other. The communities fought each other, trying to prove that one religion was better than the other.

Guru Nanak did not want people to fight. He taught that 'There is neither a Hindu nor a Muslim'. This means that God cares only for how people behave towards others and not whether they say they are a Hindu, a Muslim, a Jew, a Christian or a Sikh. As all people are God's children, serving others is serving God. It is how people act that makes them good or evil.

In this painting Guru Nanak is explaining to his followers that there is only one God. ▲

◀ *This painting shows Guru Nanak serving food to the holy men he met on his way to market. Sikhs are forbidden to worship pictures or statues, so paintings of Guru Nanak are not regarded as holy objects in themselves.*

What do Sikhs believe?

Guru Nanak taught that there is one God, who created the universe. God is always present and is everywhere. God was not born and will not die. Guru Nanak wrote the *'Mool Mantar'*, or basic teachings, which sum up Sikh beliefs about God. The *Guru Granth Sahib* begins with the *'Mool Mantar'*:

> *There is one and only one God*
> *Whose name is Truth.*
> *God the creator is without fear,*
> *without hate, immortal,*
> *without form and is beyond birth*
> *and death. And is understood through*
> *God's grace.* (*Guru Granth Sahib* page 1)

Ik Onkar means 'one God'. ▲
Some Sikhs keep this symbol in their homes to remind them of the Sikh teaching of one God.

Sikhs believe that as God has created all humans beings, everyone is equal. No one person is more important than any other.

During Guru Nanak's time, women were treated badly and were considered to be lower than men. But Guru Nanak taught:

"How can we call women bad, when great people are born from them?"
(*Guru Granth Sahib* page 473)

▲ *Balwinder Kaur is reading the **Guru Granth Sahib** at the end of the service. Men and women are equal in Sikhism. Women take part in all the **gurdwara** services, and may conduct any ceremony such as a marriage or funeral.*

When a Sikh girl is born she is given the title *'Kaur'* which means princess. This shows that a woman is an individual in her own right. She does not have to take her father's name, or later, her husband's name when she marries.

Both Sikh men and women are required to work in the kitchen at the **gurdwara**. This is to show that house work and looking after the family is a duty to be shared between men and women.
◀

Sikh *gurdwaras* are open to anyone, whatever their colour, gender or religion. Everyone is welcome to join the service, or help with the preparation of the *langar* meal. After the service everyone eats *langar* together.

Sikhs respect all religions. The *Guru Granth Sahib* even includes the writings of Hindu and Muslim saints.

▲ The foundation stone of the Golden Temple in Amritsar, one of the holiest Sikh **gurdwaras**, was laid by a Muslim saint.

The first five Gurus

Guru Nanak was the first in a line of Gurus who practised Sikh teachings, and showed people the importance of defending their beliefs. He chose his successor, Guru Angad Dev and each of the Gurus who followed were chosen by the previous Guru. Sikhs believe that the Gurus' spirits were like candles which were lit from each other.

All the Gurus provided the leadership which allowed the Sikh community to grow and develop. In doing this, some of them had to suffer a lot of hardship and two had to die to defend their beliefs.

Guru Angad Dev (1539-1552) improved the *Gurmukhi* script for writing Panjabi. *Gurmukhi* means 'from the mouth of the Guru'. At that time in India, ordinary people were forbidden to read or write Sanskrit the language which was used by priests. As all the Gurus wrote in Panjabi, their message became available for everyone to read for themselves.

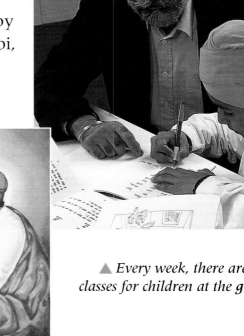

▲ *Every week, there are Panjabi classes for children at the* **gurdwara**.

◀ *This painting shows Guru Angad writing* **Gurmuki** *script.*

Guru Amar Das (1552-1574), the third Guru, divided the growing Sikh community into groups to spread the Gurus' message. He told people it was important to meet and eat *langar* together. He began celebrating the Sikh festivals of *Baisakhi* and *Diwali* at his home town of Goindwal in Punjab, so that he could meet his followers personally.

Guru Ram Das (1574-1581), the fourth Guru, founded the city of Amritsar. He composed many *shabads* or hymns, including 'Lavan', the central part of the Sikh marriage ceremony.

Guru Arjan Dev (1581-1606), the fifth Guru, built the *Harimandir Sahib* which is now known as the *Golden Temple*. He collected the writings of the four Gurus, his own and those of many Hindu and Muslim saints into the *Adi Granth*, which became the *Guru Granth Sahib*.

Emperor Jahangir tried to force Guru Arjan Dev to become a Muslim and told him to write his praises in the *Guru Granth Sahib*. When the Guru refused, he was tortured to death.

◀ *Guru Arjan was tortured in the fierce heat of June in India by being forced to sit on a hot plate while hot sand was poured over him.*

The second five Gurus

After the *martyrdom* of Guru Arjan, Sikhs had to think about how to be strong and defend their religion.

Guru Hargobind (1606-1644), the sixth Guru, became Guru after the *martyrdom* of his father. He realised that Sikhs needed to defend themselves from the rulers who wanted everyone to become a Muslim. Guru Hargobind wore two swords (look at the picture of him on p19), one as a symbol of the spiritual power of God's Truth and the other to show the importance of worldly power to defend the weak and the helpless.

Guru Har Rai (1644-1661), the seventh Guru, is well known for his kind nature. He opened free hospitals and gave away medicines to the sick and the needy.

◀ *Guru Harkrishan serving the sick.*

Guru Harkrishan (1661-1664), the eighth Guru, became the Guru at the age of five. He is remembered for the way in which he cared for sick people, without a thought for his own health. He died of smallpox when he was eight years old.

Guru Tegh Bahadur (1664-1675), the ninth Guru, lived during difficult times when the Emperor Aurengzeb was killing all Hindus who refused to become Muslims. The Guru believed that everybody should be free to worship God in the way they believed was right. When the Hindu priests asked for the Guru's help to stop this persecution of Islam, he readily agreed but then he was arrested by the Emperor's soldiers and killed.

Guru Gobind Singh (1675-1708), the tenth Guru, had to fight many battles to defend his community. He gave *amrit* on the first *Baisakhi day* and asked his Sikhs to wear the *five Ks* (see pages 20 and 21).

Before Guru Gobind Singh died, he asked his Sikhs to follow the teachings written in the ▲
Guru Granth Sahib *as their Guru.*

The Guru Granth Sahib

The writings in the *Guru Granth Sahib* are called *gurbani*, meaning 'the word of the Guru'. Sikhs believe that the *Guru Granth Sahib* is the living voice of the Gurus and that God's Truth is written in its pages.

Every copy of the *Guru Granth Sahib* is exactly the same. Each copy has 1430 pages and the same hymns are to be found on the same page in every version. English translations are available for non-Panjabi readers, but they never replace the original Panjabi version.

The whole of the *Guru Granth Sahib* is written in poetry. All the *shabads* or hymns, are set to music so that they can be sung. The hymns praise God, and tell us what God is like. They also give advice on how to lead a good life.

The children noticed the beautifully-carved canopy above the **Guru Granth Sahib**, and admired the richly-decorated cloths.

The *Guru Granth Sahib* is used for all Sikh services, festivals and ceremonies. It takes the place of a living Guru among Sikhs, so they treat it with the great respect which would have been shown to the ten human Gurus. While the *Guru Granth Sahib* is open, it is kept covered in cloths called *romallas*. It rests on cushions on a platform, and someone always sits in attendance. Then, when it has been closed, it is carefully put away. Sikhs do not worship the *Guru Granth Sahib*, but respect the teachings written in it.

On festivals and other special occasions the *Guru Granth Sahib* is read non-stop from beginning to end. This is called *Akhand Path*. *Akhand Path* takes about 48 hours. People read it in turn, reading for no more than two hours at a time.

When the *Guru Granth Sahib* is not read continuously, the reading is called *Sehaj Path*.

▲ *Giani ji is standing in attendance and waving a fan called a* **chauri** *over the* **Guru Granth Sahib**.

Mr Singh explained that the **chauri** *is a symbol of the importance of the* **Guru Granth Sahib**, *as a* **chauri** *would have been waived over kings in India. The platform, the canopy and the waving of the* **chauri** *all show* ◄ *respect to the* **Guru Granth Sahib**.

This family is praying with their friends at home in the presence of the **Guru Granth Sahib**. ▼

Many Sikhs have their own copy of the *Guru Granth Sahib* at home. Because of its importance they do not put it in an ordinary bookcase but keep it in a special place of its own. This place then becomes a *gurdwara* because the *Guru Granth Sahib* is kept there.

How do Sikhs worship?

There is no special day for Sikh worship. The *gurdwara* is open every day and people can call in to pray. The main service is held on Sunday morning, because this is a convenient time for most people. The service lasts from 8 a.m. to 2.30 p.m. People are not expected to stay for the whole time, or to be there at the beginning or at the end. The services are held in Panjabi, which is the spoken language of most of the Sikhs who come to the *gurdwara*.

*These Sikh children are bowing before the **Guru Granth Sahib** to show their respect for the teachings written in it.*

People enter the prayer hall having removed their shoes and covered their heads. They walk along the carpet in the centre of the hall towards the *Guru Granth Sahib*. They bow or kneel and leave offerings of money and sometimes of food.

They sit on the floor to show that everyone is equal, and that the *Guru Granth Sahib* is of the greatest importance in the room. Usually men and women sit down on opposite sides of the room. This is an Indian custom; there are no religious rules about it.

The service is not led by any one person in particular. Any Sikh man or woman who can read the *Guru Granth Sahib* can lead the services.

In this *gurdwara*, there is a *granthi* who is also called *Giani ji*. He is employed by the *gurdwara* to read from the *Guru Granth Sahib* and lead the prayers.

◄ *Next to the **Guru Granth Sahib**, on a lower stage sit the **ragis** who play Indian drums (called tabla), and harmonium, and sing **shabads** from the **Guru Granth Sahib**.*

The Sikh act of worship remembers and praises God. It includes *kirtan*, the singing of hymns from the *Guru Granth Sahib* and from other writings of the Gurus.

People give talks which explain the scriptures or tell stories from the lives of the Gurus. Social or political issues which affect the community are often discussed. Sometimes the talks are in English so that young people who have been born and brought up in this country can understand the issues better.

◀ At the end of the service, the congregation stands to listen to the **ardas**.

The service ends with the *ardas*, a prayer. People stand and listen to the prayer with their hands folded. In this prayer, Sikhs remember God, the Gurus and the Sikh martyrs. They ask for God's blessings on the whole of humanity. Prayers are also said for people who are sick.

After the prayer, the whole congregation sits down and the *hukam* (sometimes called *vak*) is read. *Hukam* is the seeking of guidance from the Guru. The *granthi* opens the *Guru Granth Sahib* at random and reads out a *shabad*, which is the Guru's guidance or message for the day.

*At the end of the service everyone receives the **krah prashad**, a sweet made with equal quantities of sugar, butter, flour and water. People receive this with cupped hands, to show respect for the sanctified food. This eating together shows that all people are equal.* ▶

Downstairs from the prayer hall is a large hall where people eat *langar* after every Sikh service. Each week members of different families take turns to prepare and serve food. The food is always vegetarian so that people who do not eat meat can also eat it. The food is given free.

*Harpreet Singh and Baljit Kaur have prepared the **langar** to celebrate their daughter's birthday.*

This eating together in the *langar* dates from Guru Nanak's time. In India during that period the *caste system* was followed according to strict rules. People who considered themselves to have been born into a high class refused to eat with people whom they thought belonged to a lower class.

But Guru Nanak taught that everyone is equal and should eat together as members of the big family of God.

*People eating in the **langar** ▶ hall after the service.*

Sikh Festivals

Festivals are called *gurpurabs*, which mean 'days in the honour of the Guru'. Many *gurpurabs* celebrate the births and *martyrdoms* of the Gurus. Others mark the days on which members of the Gurus' families and other Sikhs died defending the Sikh religion.

Every festival is celebrated with *Akhand Path* which is completed on the morning of the festival day. This is followed by the usual service which includes speeches about the importance of the *gurpurab*. After the service people share *langar*. To celebrate a *gurpurab*, Sikhs give money and other offerings to charity.

▶ *During this gurpurab, the **Guru Granth Sahib** was carried through the streets on a decorative float.*

The birthdays of Guru Nanak and Guru Gobind Singh

Sikhs celebrate these *gurpurabs* with street processions. The *Guru Granth Sahib* is carried on a float covered with flowers. People called the *Panj piare* (see page 21) lead the procession. The congregation follow the float and sing hymns written by the Guru. Schoolchildren play musical instruments and young people give a martial arts display. Passers-by are usually given food as a way of joining in the celebrations.

Diwali

Diwali means 'festival of lights'. On *Diwali* day Sikhs celebrate Guru Hargobind's arrival in Amritsar after his release from prison.

Guru Hargobind was imprisoned for 18 years by the Emperor Jahangir for refusing to become a Muslim. At last, impressed with the Guru's love for God and humanity, the Emperor decided to free him.

But Guru Hargobind refused to accept freedom until 52 Hindu princes who were not guilty of treason against the Emperor were also released. The Guru was told that as many princes as could pass through the narrow gate of the prison holding on to his cloak could go free. At this the Guru asked for a cloak with 52 tassels. By each holding on to one of the tassels, all the princes managed to leave the jail.

In this painting, Guru Hargobind is shown coming out of prison followed by the 52 princes.

The five Ks of Sikhism

Baisakhi, the spring festival which falls on 13 April, is celebrated by Sikhs all over the world.

On *Baisakhi* day in 1699, a crowd of over 20,000 Sikhs had gathered to celebrate the festival. Guru Gobind Singh, with a sword in his hand, declared:

'I need a Sikh, who is willing to give his life for God and the Guru'.

A stunned silence followed the Guru's words, which he repeated twice more. After the third request, a Sikh came forward and offered himself. The Guru took him to a nearby tent and, to everyone's dismay, returned with the sword which looked as if it was dripping with blood. The Guru asked for another Sikh. He took the second volunteer to the tent and came back to ask for another. He repeated his demand three more times and three more men offered themselves.

After the Guru had taken away the five volunteers, he stayed in the tent for a long time. When he returned, all five men were with him.

The Guru explained that this was a test of their courage and willingness to die for their faith and the Guru.

This painting shows Guru Gobind Singh asking for a Sikh volunteer to give his life 'for God and the Guru'.

Guru Gobind Singh called the five volunteers *Panj piare* which means 'five beloved ones'. Then the Guru prepared *amrit,* a special mixture of sugar and water. He stirred the *amrit* with a *Khanda,* the two-edged sword, while reciting *shabads,* or hymns.

▶ *On Baisakhi day, the* **Nishan Sahib** *is renewed. The flag post is taken down and washed, the flag and the cloth covering the pole are replaced.*

The men and women who took *amrit* on *Baisakhi* day in 1699 were asked to wear the five symbols as the uniform of Sikhism. These are:

Kes - un-cut hair, to show saintliness.

Kanga - a small wooden comb, worn in the hair to keep the hair clean.

Kara - an iron or steel bracelet, reminding Sikhs to do good deeds.

Kacch - shorts, which are easy to wear, symbolising an active life.

Kirpan - a sword, reminding Sikhs of their duty to defend the weak.

▲ *Mr Singh showed the children the 5 Ks which make up the uniform of Sikhism.*

◀ *Gagandeep Singh's mother combs his un-cut hair.*

Family celebrations

For Sikhs family life is very important. Guru Nanak writes:

'Living within the family one finds God' *(Guru Granth Sahib page 661).*

The special times in a Sikh's life are celebrated in the *gurdwara* in the presence of the *Guru Granth Sahib*. All the celebrations follow the usual service and *langa* is always served at the end of each ceremony.

When a baby is born, the family welcomes the baby as a gift from God and celebrates this at the naming ceremony.

After the usual service, when the *Guru Granth Sahib* is opened for *hukam*, the baby's name is chosen to begin with the first letter of the first word of the *shabad*.

As soon as the members of the family decide on the name, they announce it to the congregation.

Jasjit and Jatinder are taking part in a service to name their baby daughter. The first letter of her name is to be 'D'.

Most Sikh names are used for both boys and girls. Take the name Simran, for example. A boy would be called Simran *Singh* and a girl would be Simran *Kaur*. The use of *Singh* and *Kaur* in a Sikh name shows whether it belongs to male or female. *Singh* means 'lion' - this shows the need for people to be hol and brave to defend the weak. *Kaur* means 'princess' - this is a symbol of how the Sikh religion gave women a higher status in life than they had had before.

Before young Sikh boys start wearing a turban they keep their un-cut hair tied in a top knot under a *patka*. Some boys wear a small handkerchief called a *roomal*; others may plait their hair.

◀

*Ravneet Singh and Arjandeep Singh are having their turbans tied for the first time in the presence of the **Guru Granth Sahib**. Their uncles are tying the turbans.*

Sometimes when a young boy ties his turban for the first time, a special ceremony is held at the *gurdwara*. This usually takes place when a boy is about ten or eleven, often just before he starts secondary school.

During the usual service, just before the *ardas* is said, a member of the family, a friend or a *granthi* ties the turban on the boy's head. An adult turban is usually five metres long but a three metre long turban is usually used for a young boy. This is a time of great pleasure and pride for the whole family, when they celebrate that their young son is growing into manhood.

*Ravneet Singh ties his **patka** as he gets ready for school.* ▶

The *amrit* ceremony is celebrated in the presence of the *Guru Granth Sahib*. In the Hounslow Gurdwara, the ceremony takes place during the *Baisakhi* festival. Anyone who is committed to the Sikh way of life can take *amrit*. Men or women taking *amrit* come to the ceremony wearing the *five Ks*, the uniform of Sikhism.

*The **Panj piare** prepare to conduct the **amrit** ceremony.* ▲

Five people conduct the service, representing the *Panj piare* who took *amrit* from Guru Gobind Singh on *Baisakhi* day in 1699. Clean water and sugar crystals are put in a steel bowl. The *Panj piare* stir the water with a *Khanda*, while reciting the five prayers. After the prayers are completed, those taking *amrit* receive it in cupped hands and drink it five times. The *amrit* is also sprinkled five times on both their hair and eyes. The ceremony ends with the usual service and *langar* is served.

During a marriage ceremony, the bride and groom sit in front of the *Guru Granth Sahib*. They listen to a speech which reminds them of their duties to each other and to the community. Then the bride's father places one end of the bridegroom's scarf, called a *pala*, in the bride's hand. This is a symbol that they are being joined together as husband and wife. The couple hold the *pala* for the rest of the ceremony.

Mona and Harinder are standing side by side in front of the **Guru Granth Sahib***, ready for the marriage ceremony to begin.* ▶

The bride and groom are walking round the **Guru Granth Sahib** *for the fourth and last time.*

▼

In the most important part of the marriage ceremony, the *granthi* reads the first verse of the *Lavan* from the *Guru Granth Sahib* and then it is sung by the *ragis*, while the couple walk round the *Guru Granth Sahib*.

When they reach their starting position they bow to the *Guru Granth Sahib* and sit down to listen to the next verse. This is repeated four times. After the service everyone eats *langar* together.

When a Sikh dies, relatives and friends try to avoid shows of grief and read the *Guru Granth Sahib* for comfort. Sikhs believe that death is like going to sleep in one world and waking up in another. During a funeral *Sehaj Path* is read, followed by the usual service. Afterwards, *langar* is served.

Sikh life

Sikhs try to lead a good life by following three basic rules. *Nam Japna* means remembering God by reading and reflecting on the Gurus' teachings written in the *Guru Granth Sahib*. Sikhs usually say their prayers in the morning and in the evening, either in the *gurdwara* or at home.

Kirat karna means earning your living by being honest and working hard. Sikhs follow the example of Bhai Lalo, a poor hard-working carpenter who lived during the time of Guru Nanak.

Bhai Lalo lived in the same village as a rich man called Bhago, who made poor people work hard for him and paid them very little money. Guru Nanak went to stay with Lalo. 'Why don't you stay with me?' Bhago asked the Guru. Guru Nanak replied: 'Lalo's simple bread is earned by honest work. But you have grown rich by taking advantage of the poor. Your food is stained with blood.'

The story goes that the Guru took a piece of Lalo's bread in one hand and a piece of Bhago's bread in the other, and squeezed them both. Milk dripped from Lalo's bread and blood from Bhago's bread.

The rich man realised his mistake and promised to help the poor and needy.

Vand chhakna means sharing with others who are needy and *sewa* means serving God's people. *Sewa* can take many forms. It may mean giving money, working in the *gurdwara*, or looking after the sick. A Sikh should offer help to anyone who needs it.

Sikhs remember the story of Bhai Kanaya. He was brought to Guru Gobind Singh after he was seen giving water to enemy soldiers wounded in a battle between Sikhs and Muslims.

The Guru asked Bhai Kanaya to explain his actions. 'I am a water carrier', he said. 'It's my duty to take water to the wounded and the dying.'

'But he was giving water to Muslim soldiers as well,' complained the guard. Bhai Kanaya said: 'I saw no Muslims and no Sikhs, no friends and no enemies, I saw only God's people. I was practising what you taught us.'

'You are a true Sikh,' said the Guru and blessed Bhai Kanaya for his true spirit of service to God's creation.

Time-line

This time-line shows some of the most important dates in Sikh history and key events in the Sikh community in Britain up to the present day. It uses the CE (Common Era) dating system which is shared by the major religions.

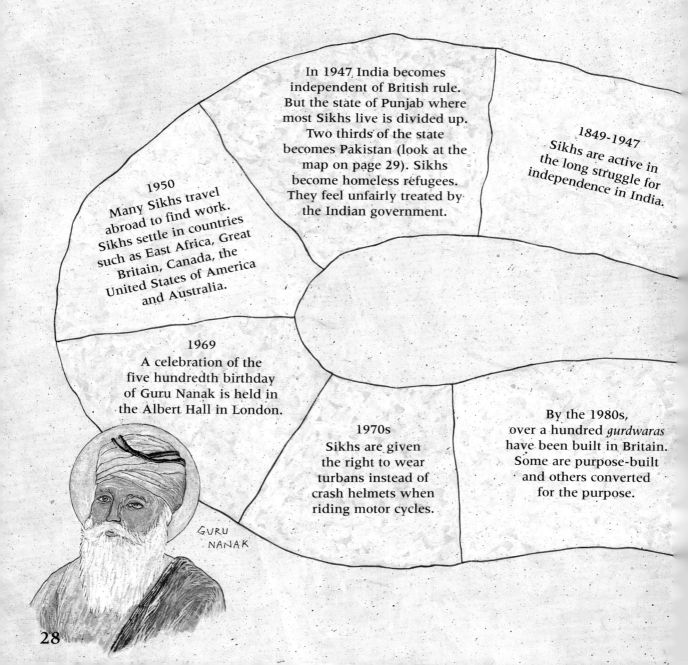

In 1947 India becomes independent of British rule. But the state of Punjab where most Sikhs live is divided up. Two thirds of the state becomes Pakistan (look at the map on page 29). Sikhs become homeless refugees. They feel unfairly treated by the Indian government.

1849-1947
Sikhs are active in the long struggle for independence in India.

1950
Many Sikhs travel abroad to find work. Sikhs settle in countries such as East Africa, Great Britain, Canada, the United States of America and Australia.

1969
A celebration of the five hundredth birthday of Guru Nanak is held in the Albert Hall in London.

1970s
Sikhs are given the right to wear turbans instead of crash helmets when riding motor cycles.

By the 1980s, over a hundred *gurdwaras* have been built in Britain. Some are purpose-built and others converted for the purpose.

GURU NANAK

1469 -1708
During these years the ten Gurus guide the Sikh community through times of peace and persecution. Before Guru Gobind Singh dies, he gives the Guruship to the *Guru Granth Sahib*, ending the line of human Gurus.

1708-1739
During this period Sikhs suffer much persecution. The Muslim rulers of India offer rewards to anyone who brings them the head or any part of a Sikh's body. Sikhs leave their homes and hide in jungle areas for safety.

1739-1799
Sikhs fight and defeat invaders from Afghanistan. They establish their own twelve independent states in Punjab.

MAHARAJA RANJIT SINGH

1799-1839
Maharaja Ranjit Singh is the Emperor of Punjab.

1839-1849
After the death of Maharaja Ranjit Singh, the British conquer Punjab and add it to their Indian Empire.

1799-1839
Maharaja Ranjit Singh treats people of all religions equally. Sikhs, Hindus and Muslims hold important posts in his empire.

GURDWARA SINGH SABHA

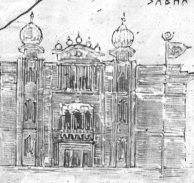

1983
A Sikh boy is refused admission to a school wearing his turban. When the case is taken to court, the House of Lords decides that Sikhs have the right to wear turbans at all times.

1984
The Indian Government attacks the Golden Temple and all the historic *gurdwaras* in Punjab. Thousands of Sikh worshippers die during the attack. The library containing the priceless original writings of the Gurus is destroyed.

Sikhs campaign for their own independent Sikh state.

1994
The *Gurdwara Singh Sabha* opens in Hounslow. It is one of the new purpose-built *gurdwaras.*

How to find out more

Visiting the gurdwara

Everyone is welcome to visit the Gurdwara Sri Guru Singh Sabha at: Alice Way (off Hanworth Road), Hounslow, Middlesex. Tel: 0208 577 2793 (Phone the gurdwara's Secretary for advice on the best time to visit.)

As with other holy places, behaviour should be respectful: tobacco and alcohol are not allowed in the *gurdwara*.

Before entering the prayer hall you will need to remove your shoes and cover your head.

To find out the location of your nearest Sikh *gurdwara*, look in the places of worship section of the telephone directory, or contact your local SACRE (Standing Advisory Council for Religious Education).

Making a collection of Sikh artefacts

Collecting artefacts and learning about their use is a good way of learning about Sikhism. *Gurdwaras* often sell artefacts and books on the day of the main service.

The Sikh Missionary Society (10 Featherstone Road Southall, Middlesex, UB2 5AA) supplies free literature and stocks artefacts which can be ordered by post. Tel: 0208-574-1902 (Phone before you visit to check the opening hours.)

For a basic collection you will need: a *gutka* which contains extracts from the *Guru Granth Sahib*, *romallas*, a *kanga*, a *kara*, a small *kirpan*, an *Ik Onkar* symbol, a *Khanda symbol*, postcards with pictures of *gurdwaras* or writings from the *Guru Granth Sahib* and pictures of the Gurus.

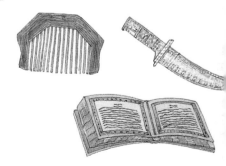

Useful Words

Akhand Path The continuous reading of the *Guru Granth Sahib*.

Amrit A word meaning 'nectar'. *Amrit* is made by stirring sugar crystals into water with a *Khanda* while reciting passages from the Sikh scriptures.

Ardas A formal prayer offered at all religious services and ceremonies.

Chauri A fan made of yak hair or nylon, waved over the *Guru Granth Sahib* to show respect for it.

Five Ks The symbols of Sikhism worn by both men and women.

Giani One who is learned in the Sikh scriptures. The title is used for a *granthi* and a *ragi*.

Granthi A reader of the *Guru Granth Sahib*, who may also lead a ceremony.

Gurdwara A Sikh place of worship.

Gurmukhi 'From the Guru's mouth'; the name given to the script in which the scriptures are written in the Panjabi language.

Gurpurabs Major events in the Sikh calendar connected with the lives of the Gurus.

Guru Granth Sahib The collection of Sikh scriptures compiled by Guru Arjan and declared as the Guru by Guru Gobind Singh.

hukam A reading taken at random for guidance from the *Guru Granth Sahib*. The word means 'God's will'.

Ik Onkar A symbol meaning 'there is only one God'.

Kaur A name meaning 'princess' given to every female Sikh.

Khanda A double-edged sword used in the *amrit* ceremony and as the emblem on the Sikh flag.

kirat karna Earning one's livelihood by one's own efforts.

krah prashad A sweet food made with equal quantities of flour or semolina, sugar, and butter or ghee (purified butter). It is shared at the end of Sikh gatherings to symbolise equality.

langar The *gurdwara* dining hall and the food served in it. The word means 'Guru's kitchen'

Lavan The part of the marriage ceremony during which the couple walk round the *Guru Granth Sahib*. It is also the name of the marriage hymn.

martyrdom The deaths of the Gurus and others for Sikh principles.

Nam Japna Remembering God by reading and reflecting on the *Guru Granth Sahib*.

Nishan Sahib The Sikh flag, flown at *gurdwaras* and other Sikh buildings.

pala A scarf held by the groom and the bride during a wedding.

Panj piare The 'five beloved ones'; the first five Sikhs to be given *amrit* by Guru Gobind Singh.

patka A head covering used by boys before they start wearing a turban.

ragis Sikh musicians who sing compositions from the *Guru Granth Sahib*.

romallas The cloths used to cover the *Guru Granth Sahib*.

roomal A head covering worn by young boys.

Sehaj Path A complete reading of the *Guru Granth Sahib*.

sewa A word meaning 'service'; an essential part of the life of every Sikh.

shabads Hymns from the *Guru Granth Sahib*.

Singh A word meaning 'lion'. A name used by all Sikh males.

vand chhakna The sharing of a person's time, talents and earnings with less fortunate people.

Index

Reprinted 2002, 2005, 2007
First paperback edition 2000

First published 1998
A & C Black Publishers Ltd
38 Soho Square, London W1D 3HB
www.acblack.com

ISBN 978-0-7136-5496-7

© A & C Black Publishers Ltd

A CIP catalogue record for this book is available from the British Library.

Acknowledgements
The author and publisher would like to thank Indarjit Singh OBE, editor of the Sikh Messenger and Director of the Network of Organisations for his advice. We would also like to thank everyone concerned with the Gurdwara and the staff and children of Orchard Junior School, particularly Damian, Chirag, Rebecca, Rupa and Vandna for their help in the preparation of this book.

All photographs by Zul Mukhida except for pp3a, 21a TRIP Photo Library; pp 4, 5, 8b, 9(both), 11(both), 19, 20, 23a, 25(both), 26, 27 *Sikh Messenger* Publications and Ramgarhia Sabha Southall; pp18, 24 David Rose.

All artwork by Vanessa Card

Printed in China by WKT Co. Ltd

A & C Black uses paper produced from elemental chlorine-free pulp, harvested from managed, sustainable forests.